WISDOM TREE

Contents

1. **Freedom**   **3**

   For to be free is not merely to cast off one's chains, but to live in a way that respects and enhances the freedom of others.

2. **Simplicity**   **11**

   In character, in manner, in style, in all things, the supreme excellence is simplicity.

3. **Peace**   **21**

   "Peace begins with a smile."

4. **Positivity**   **32**

   "If you think you can do a thing, or you think you can't do a thing, you're always right."

5. **Compassion**   **40**

   Compassion is never forgotten. It changes the world and makes it a better place.

6. **Determination**   **51**

   "Our greatest glory is not in never falling but in rising every time we fall."

7. **Open Mindedness**   **61**

   Intolerance stems from the inability to be open-minded.

   Analyzing Myself   **71**

Freedom

What is freedom?
Freedom is the power to act, speak and think as one wants without any fear or restrictions. Freedom is being free in body and in mind. It is the capacity to think on one's own, according to one's own outlook and do as he or she wishes without being subjected to any form of pressure. It is the state of not being imprisoned by walls. It is also the state of not being a slave to someone or something. Freedom is extremely essential for human beings to realize their full potential and progress both as an individual and as a community.

Let us learn a bit more about freedom from Rabindranath Tagore's famous poem.

Where The Mind Is Without Fear

Where the mind is without fear and the head is held high

Where knowledge is free

Where the world has not been broken up into fragments

By narrow domestic walls

Where words come out from the depth of truth

Where tireless striving stretches its arms towards perfection

Where the clear stream of reason has not lost its way

Into the dreary desert sand of dead habit

Where the mind is led forward by thee

Into ever-widening thought and action

Into that heaven of freedom, my Father, let my country awake.

— Rabindranath Tagore

Let us understand more about Rabindranath Tagore's vision of freedom for India. True freedom he says is attained when people do not dwell with fear in their minds. Freedom is the state of being proud of one's existence and

one's identity. A country is truly free when all its citizens are given opportunity to gain knowledge freely. True freedom demands the eradication of all kinds of boundaries and walls that separate people from one another.

Freedom is also the ability to show integrity and values. When people speak the truth and are willing to work hard to do the best they can do, they are indeed free. When people are capable of thinking with reason and do not lead their lives and thought by mere habit, they are indeed free. Freedom is also governed and defined by the ability to think progressively and act accordingly.

Comprehension questions

Answer the following questions to test your understanding of the story.

1. In your own words describe why you think the poet says that in a truly free land, people should be without fear in their minds.

   _____
   _____
   _____

2. What do you think the poet is referring to through the words 'fragments…narrow domestic walls'?

   _____
   _____
   _____

3. Name any two attributes that according to Rabindranath Tagore ought to be displayed by people living in a free land.

   _____
   _____
   _____

4. How does he describe 'habit' in the poem?

   _____
   _____
   _____

5. Why does the poet use the word 'awake'? What can you say about the state of the poet's country by this last line in the poem?

_____

_____

_____

More about the Value

> "Freedom is my birthright and I shall have it." — Bal Gangadhar Tilak

Freedom from foreign rule, freedom from tyranny, freedom from regressive thoughts and freedom from oppression are some of the kinds of freedoms that people have always sought after.

As recent as just over a half a century, people in India, the largest democracy in the world were fighting for political freedom. They wanted to govern themselves and not be under foreign leadership.

What then is freedom? Whether it is foreign rule or a self-rule, the common man is still governed by someone else. So how is he or she free?

Freedom is never complete freedom. No person can be free to do whatever he or she wishes. One has to remember that one is living in a society and has no right to hurt someone else.

After all, they say,

> My freedom ends where the other person's nose begins.

This means, while one is free to do or think the way he wants, he has to still think about others and their welfare. Everyone has to abide by the rules of the society they are living in, and their freedom has to be defined by these rules.

Sometimes, the rules of the society may seem unfair. At times like these, people come together and try to change the rule and the way the society functions. This is what happened during the freedom struggle in India and some other countries too. People did not like the way a foreign rule was imposed on them, and so they came together to change this scenario. Another example where people came together was to eradicate racism and apartheid in USA and Africa and 'untouchability' in India.

A VALUE FOR ME

For to be free is not merely to cast off one's chains, but to live in a way that respects and enhances the freedom of others.

Snippet

Martin Luther King Jr was an African American who worked for racial equality in America. He also worked for civil rights in the country. The following poem gives us an insight into what he considers freedom for people of the world.

One Day…
Youngsters will learn words they will
Not understand.

Children from India will ask:
What is hunger?
Children from Alabama will ask:
What is racial segregation?
Children from Hiroshima will ask:
What is the atomic bomb?
Children at school will ask:
What is war?

You will answer them.
You will tell them:

Those words are not used anymore,
Like stage coaches, galleys or
Slavery.
Words no longer meaningful.

That is why they have been
Removed from dictionaries.

— Martin Luther King

Exercises

1. **Paste pictures of any eight people from across the globe who have fought for freedom of different kinds. Mention in a couple of words what they have fought for.**

_____

_____

_____

_____

_____

2. **India grants its citizens certain kinds of freedoms. They are popularly called the 'Seven Freedoms.' Identify all seven of them in the word grid below.**

a	s	s	o	c	i	a	t	i	o	n	u	y
b	e	x	p	r	e	s	s	i	o	n	t	r
q	t	t	y	r	s	f	h	n	x	i	n	p
a	t	h	a	a	o	e	y	y	r	l	e	y
w	l	g	t	d	v	p	r	o	d	s	m	i
f	e	f	c	y	c	z	e	p	v	m	e	d
i	m	b	s	q	t	o	f	r	s	d	v	f
j	e	n	o	c	c	u	p	a	t	i	o	n
h	n	a	a	s	s	e	m	b	l	y	m	i
c	t	n	b	m	r	d	b	s	w	c	v	n

3. **'Freedom within the boundaries of law.'**

   Write down at least six scenarios where you would consider freedom without breaking any law. The first one has been done for you to help you along with the others.

   a. Every person in India has the right to practice a religion of his or her choice. However, this does not mean that they can abuse other faith and be disrespectful to people of other faith. This also does not mean that they could impose their faith on others.

   b. _____
   _____
   _____
   _____

   c. _____
   _____
   _____
   _____

d. _____
_____
_____

e. _____
_____
_____
_____

f. _____
_____
_____
_____

4. **Research Activity:**

   In a previous activity, we have identified some of the freedoms granted to people by India. Do you think these kinds of freedoms are enjoyed by people all over the world? Do you agree that these freedoms are essential to human progress, tolerance and peace? Why or why not? Write an essay in not less than 800 words and share your views with your classmates.

Test yourself

1. Do you think it is okay for people to follow any religion of their choice as long as it does not harm others?
2. Do you like the system of democracy where people vote for their leader?
3. Do you find it unfair that people who are only 18 or above get a driving license?
4. Do you insist on your friends agreeing with everything you say?
5. Do you protest when your parents ask you to sleep early every night? Do you believe that you should be given the freedom to sleep when you wish to?

*If your answers to questions 1 and 2 are 'yes', then you are an advocate of freedom. Else, you need to work on changing your attitude to respect the concept of freedom. Accept the fact that everyone deserves freedom and understand that freedom comes with responsibility and a bit of restraint. This restraint is generally in the form of self-discipline. For instance, you should have the self-discipline to sleep early especially on a school day, and even otherwise, because it is healthy for you.

Tips to Parents and Teachers

Freedom comes with great responsibility. While children cannot seem to wait for freedom, it is a parent's and a teacher's duty to teach them to exercise freedom wisely. The best practice would be to start giving bits of freedom from a young age. For instance, you could discuss a choice of menu for dinner before preparing it. That way, the child will have the freedom to choose which vegetable to eat in dinner. Similarly, while preparing a list of invitees for a party, the child could be given a choice add to the list. Once this freedom has been given and exercised by the child, a discussion on the choice to should also be followed. This way, the child will be able to understand how wise or unwise his or her choice was. The child will be able to assess the implication of his or her freedom. It is better for a child to make an error at a young age and fumble with minor problems and eventually brace up for freedom attained as an adult. New found and sudden freedom is difficult to handle for anyone.

Do's and Don'ts

1. Understand rules and regulations of a school, a community or a country before showing your freedom.
2. Understand that just as you, everyone else too has a right to freedom. While expressing your freedom, you should not curtail that of another; you should not harm them in anyway.
3. Never cross the boundaries of law while expressing your freedom.
4. Make your choices wisely. Try not to make a bad and unwise decision with the freedom given to you.
5. Use your freedom with caution and with responsibility.

> For to be free is not merely to cast off one's chains, but to live in a way that respects and enhances the freedom of others.
>
> — Nelson Mandela

Simplicity

What is simplicity?
When something is easy to understand, it is considered simple. When something is easy to do, it is considered simple. Simplicity is the quality of being easy to understand and to do.

A simple person is one who is uncomplicated. He is plain in his thoughts, humble in his actions and generous too. A simple person is easy to be friends with, and is generally experienced and wise.

Simplicity in actions and thoughts is a good quality.

Let us read the following essays to understand more about simplicity.

Simplicity of Thought in the Panchatantra

The Panchatantra is a very popular collection of stories originally written in Sanskrit.

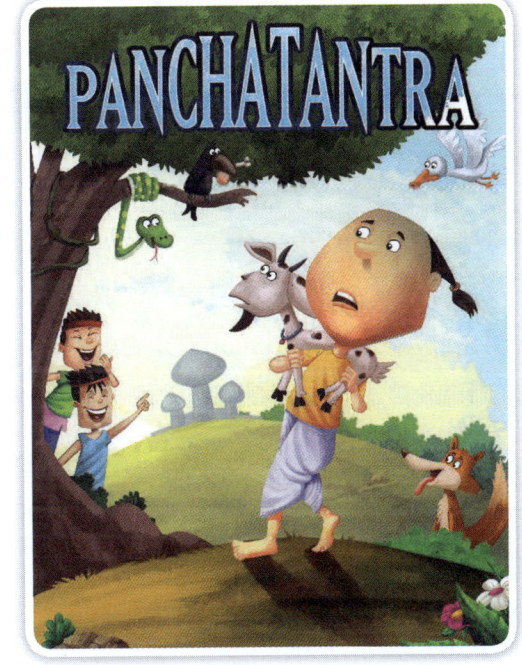

It is said that the author, Vishnu Sarma was given the task of educating four young princes. In order to help the young princes understand the ways of the world and gain wisdom enough to handle themselves in the world, the teacher decided to impart the knowledge through simple stories. Although the stories themselves seem simple and easy to understand, they are all inter related and move smoothly from one to another. Although the technique is difficult, yet it is made to look easy by a proficient writer.

While human beings figure in some stories, most of the stories have animals as the characters. The simplicity of language and plot and the choice of characters make for an interesting and effective story.

The book believed to have been written around the 3rd century BCE. It gained such popularity, mainly because of the magnitude of wisdom imparted through simple and short stories, that its fame spread far and wide throughout the ancient world. In fact, the stories of The Panchatantra are still popular even after so many centuries.

One scholar noted that there are over 200 versions of the book written in over 50 languages of the world, where a majority of these languages are not native to

India. It has been translated into languages ranging from Persian and Arabic to Greek, Latin, German, English and even old Slavonic.

The Panchatantra is also considered by many to be the inspiration behind many stories in the Aesop's Fables, Arabian Nights, Sindbad and even some popular western nursery rhymes and ballads.

Simplicity of Design in Modern Gadgets

Have you ever worked on a desktop computer? Have you ever handled a laptop or a smart phone? Have you ever given the design of a computer or the smart phone any thought? Did the complexity involved in constructing such a small device that can do such a multitude of activities ever boggle you?

We may all take the workings of our modern gadgets like the telephone, a smart phone, a television or even a space vehicle near Pluto for granted. To a child born in this century, all these may seem a cakewalk.

The concept of electricity, the ability to tackle deadly diseases with immunizations and the ability to travel around the world within hours are all matters that are hardly pondered over.

However, for these things to become a reality and for these things to seem so simple and easy, it took several extraordinary people, several decades and centuries to accomplish.

Though the result looks simple, yet the effort to arrive at simplicity is tremendous.

Simplicity in actions, thoughts and speech is what should be aimed at.

Comprehension questions

Answer the following questions to test your understanding of the essays.

1. What are some of the specialties in the narrative technique of The Panchatantra?

2. How can you measure the popularity of The Panchatantra?

3. Name some of the works of literature that were inspired by The Panchatantra.

4. Why would the working of a complex gadget like a smart phone or an unmanned vehicle in space seem normal to a child born in this century?

5. How did such complex gadgets as are mentioned in the esays above come to be so simple in look and have an ease of functioning?

More about the Value

Simplicity as we understand is how something is said or done in such an easy way that everyone understands it and uses it with ease. There is no complication or confusion involved when things are said with simplicity and done with simplicity.

That was with regards to simplicity of action. What do we understand about simplicity of thoughts? Simplicity in thought is not a mark of poor thought. On the other hand, thoughts that are formed from deep thoughts, wisdom, experience and confidence are often simple. They are easy to emulate and give better solutions to problems at hand.

How about simplicity in lifestyle? Gandhiji once said, "Simplicity is a matter of the heart…. the ideal is not to possess anything which the poorest on earth does not." There is no better example to be seen in recent years than the father of our nation. He was a man of simple means; he did not have many personal possessions. Yet, his thoughts were so exalted that he lead the freedom movement in one of the largest countries in the world and inspired many other nations and leaders to think about peaceful and non-violent ways in which to lead life and win freedom. Let us

read the following snippet to know more about Gandhiji, the man who believed in 'simple living and high thinking.'

"Simplicity is the ultimate sophistication."
— Leonardo da Vinci

"Nature is pleased with simplicity."
— Isaac Newton

A VALUE FOR ME

In character, in manner, in style, in all things, the supreme excellence is simplicity.

Snippet

It is said that when Gandhiji died, he had very few personal possessions. So few were they, that one could count them using his or her fingers. He had only a watch, spectacles, sandals and eating bowl.

Gandhiji was born into a wealthy family in current day Gujarat. His family was prosperous enough to get him educated in England. After studying law at the University College in London, he held a good job in Africa. So one might wonder why a person from a well off family and with enough qualifications to fend for himself died such a poor man.

The reason is that it was a choice Gandhiji made. The man who wore nothing but a dhoti and another piece of cloth to cover his upper body, is recognized and remembered world over for his thoughts, actions, principles and teachings.

> "Manifest plainness, Embrace simplicity,
> Reduce selfishness, Have few desires."
> — Lao Tzu

Exercises

1. Hidden in the word grid below are eight words. They are synonyms or antonyms of the word simplicity. Locate the words. Circle the synonyms in green and the antonyms in red. This exercise will help you test your understanding of the word simplicity.

W	K	A	S	T	B	A	S	K	B	O	R	I	N	G	B
F	A	M	I	S	U	T	Y	I	E	C	D	R	I	G	N
V	Z	W	E	V	E	R	D	I	A	C	G	Y	J	H	I
P	R	E	T	E	N	T	I	O	U	S	I	M		C	M
L	D	I	F	F	I	C	U	L	T	Y	N	A	C	D	B
O	G	R	W	E	E	V	B	N	I	M	T	T	L	S	L
D	S	T	R	A	I	G	H	T	F	O	R	W	A	R	D
U	G	H	S	R	W	Z	T	F	U	H	O	I	R	X	A
M	R	T	H	A	H	C	Y	P	L	A	I	N	I	S	S
L	I	V	H	E	N	M	R	T	U	S	N	N	T	Q	T
A	B	I	S	K	U	R	T	E	O	U	I	E	Y	A	E
R	S	H	A	R	C	O	M	P	L	E	X	I	T	Y	D

2. Make a list of things in your house that you have not made use of in the past six months. Once your list is ready, identify carefully whether you can do away with anything on this list? Are they really essential in your life? Can you not live without them?

_____

_____

_____

_____

_____

_____

Accumulating things is not a sign of prosperity. Being able to decide what to have and what not to have; being able to share what you have with others who need it; being able to think of others in all your actions; and being able to discard what you do not need will enable you to live a better and simpler life.

Simplicity does not mean living frugally or in a miserly fashion. Simplicity means being able to de-clutter your life.

3. **Simple things are often easy to understand and remember. Below are the names of some simple things. They may be simple, yet they are very important, full of meaning and extremely essential in our world.**

   Supply a suitable word to complete the names. A clue or two has been given along with each name. The words are also provided in the box below. They are, however, jumbled up.)

   | platbhae | helew | speaso | net | ripmary | moat |

   a. _____ Fables (They are simple stories but full of wisdom. There wouldn't be a person around you who hasn't read or heard some of these fables.)

   b. _____ Colours (Just three in number, yet the multitude of colours that you can imagine are all created from these basic colours.)

   c. Structure of an _____ (They are considered the basic building blocks of all matter. They are very tiny and yet many of them together become large things.)

   d. _____ digits (They may be a handful and yet they can represent countless numbers.)

   e. The _____ (It helps in easy movement. It is definitely one of the most important inventions that helped in the advancement of all civilizations the world over.)

   f. Twenty six special symbols of the _____. They are the building blocks of our written communication.

4. **Research, meditate and arrive at a conclusion / decision.**

   Though people all over the world are similar, they do not have equal opportunities. Those living in richer countries have a better lifestyle and those living in poorer countries have a poorer lifestyle. Those living in richer countries have better access to more nutritional foods while those in poorer countries make do with what is available. Choose any one developed country and one underdeveloped country. Gather the following parameters and then compare and contrast.

Parameters	Developed Country ( )	Underdeveloped Country ( )
Population		
Density of population		
Life Expectancy		
Per Capita Income		
Rate of Unemployment		
Main Source of Income		

Do you find it unfair or unjust that one country suffers while another prospers? Do you think moderate use of resources by all, irrespective of their purchasing power will help in leveling out this difference in the world? Express your views on the same by citing what people can do to lead a simpler life so as to ensure that our resources are shared, not depleted and more importantly not wasted.

_____
_____
_____
_____
_____
_____
_____
_____
_____
_____

5. The following words suggest ways in which simplicity can be achieved. However, these words have all been scrambled up. Unscramble them to read the suggestions.

   a. crelecy
   b. pu cycel
   c. eoc frindeyl leifestyl
   d. ipoistvity
   e. contnetnetm
   f. dectluter
   g. ste pu routenis
   h. deruction

Test yourself

Are you a happy person? Answer the following questions and check for yourself. Be truthful while answering the questions.

1. Do you answer to the point when you are asked something?
2. Do you keep your room cluttered?
3. When going on a trip, do you insist on travelling light?
4. Do you like to accumulate books and toys (even those you don't read or play with)?
5. Do you like to have elaborate theme parties on your birthdays?

If the answers to the questions 2, 3 and 5 are 'yes', then you need to rethink your lifestyle. You may want to think more about simplicity. Remember, people will know you and remember you by your thoughts and your actions and not by what you own.

> "A vocabulary of truth and simplicity will be of service throughout your life."
> — Winston Churchill

Tips to Parents and Teachers

Albert Einstein once said, "If you can't explain it to a six year old, you don't understand it yourself." Therefore, simple things are often most understood, most appreciated and most effective. Encourage children to think deeply. Deep thoughts bring about clarity of concept. With clarity of concept comes simplicity in actions and communication.

Simplicity in life is something that we can teach children through practicing it ourselves. Discuss the concept of sharing. In today's commercial world, it is not uncommon to have children demanding a list of things for themselves. These can range from a personal cell phone to a television in their room and so on. Teach them that there is an alternative way of living in which a family can share one television or computer. When things can be shared, they ought to be shared. Similarly, encourage them to think twice before spending on anything. They need to learn to assess the difference between need and greed before acquiring something for themselves.

Dos and Don'ts

1. It is good to have a large and impressive vocabulary. But your big words only when they are required. Your sentences should be easy to read and understand and not a display of your vocabulary.
2. Hoarding things at your home is not a sign of prosperity. Have only those things that you really require.
3. When you can make something for yourself, do so. Do not insist on buying such stuff.
4. Make your own toys and learn to share them with others. When you share your toys and books, you grow richer in experience and never poorer.
5. There is no shame in using recycled or upcycled things. You are saving the planet by doing so.
6. Simplicity is not obtained easily. Simplicity comes about with rich experience. So, work hard to attain this.
7. Simple living, high thinking is a good motto in life.

> Simplicity is an inward realty seen in our outward lifestyle.
> — Richard Foster

Peace

What is peace?

Peace is a state of harmony and tranquility. It is not merely the absence of war as many believe it to be. Peace is the presence of justice, goodness and serenity. Every civilization throughout history has been aiming to achieve peace. Every effort by every government is to provide its citizens peace. Every individual aims at achieving inner peace for the wellbeing of his own self.

Let us read the following story to understand more about peace.

Story

Every battle has a story. There is a reason why the battle is fought. There is a reason why the battle is lost. There is a reason why the people in the battle are there to fight. Sometimes there is more than one story - that of the victor and that of the loser as well as that of each of the soldiers involved in the battle.

There is an interesting story about a battle that happened many centuries ago. The two armies fighting the war were gathered at a large battlefield. As it was the rule in those days, the fighting ensued in the morning and went on until sun set.

At the end of every day, the battle would be stalled. The wounded would be carried back to their camp to be tended to. The dead would be given a proper burial or cremation.

The two armies that were gathered at this battle field fought fiercely for many days. At the end of each day, the routine was followed. The battle was even. There was an equal number of casualties on each side.

Eventually, there was just one soldier from each army left alive on the battlefield. They fought with each other, but neither was successful in felling the other before sunset.

When the sun set, the two men decided to stop fighting and continue the next day.

With no one left in the miserable battlefield, but each other for company, they both built just one fire, huddled around it and started talking to each other.

"My son would be waiting for me at home," said one of them. "He would be playing with his wooden sword, dreaming of growing up to be a soldier like me," he said.

"I don't have a son, but I have a daughter. Every time I look at her, I see the youth of my wife. My daughter would be waiting at the door, ready with a bright smile, to greet me when I return," said the other soldier.

In this manner, they continued their conversation. They spoke of their children, their parents, their childhood, their dreams and their difficulties. They also spoke of the fields that needed to be harvested when they returned home.

Thus, they spoke for most part of the night. When the sun rose the next day, they strapped on their helmets, sheathed their swords, looked at each other, and silently turned around and went away from each other. Then they went on their own way, away from the battlefield, to their countries, to their villages; to their families.

The wise say, it is not possible to hate someone when you know their story.

Comprehension questions

Answer the following questions to test your understanding of peace.

1. What are the different kinds of stories that the author lists at the beginning of the above narration?
   _____
   _____
   _____

2. What were the rules of the battle?
   _____
   _____
   _____

3. What would the soldiers of both the camps do during the night when the battle was stalled?
   _____
   _____
   _____

4. What did the only alive soldiers do during the night?
   _____
   _____
   _____

5. Why do you think the two of them did not fight? Why do you think they walked away silently?
   _____
   _____
   _____

More about the Value

The Dalai Lama, the spiritual head of the Tibetan Buddhists, once said, "Peace does not mean the absence of conflicts." He explained that conflicts are an inevitable part of the world. It is in human nature to have conflicts. It is in human nature to have differences. However, peaceful methods of dialogue, education and knowledge have to be employed in overcoming these differences and conflicts. When this can be done without causing the other person any harm, the world will be a peaceful place.

Peace can be attained by acknowledging differences, accepting them and practicing a restraint.

Malala Yousafzai, the 17 year old Noble Peace Laureate, who braved the guns of the Taliban to get educated, said, "If you want to end the war then instead of sending guns, send books. Instead of sending tanks, send pens. Instead of sending soldiers, send teachers." This is the way to attain peace.

Peace is essential for progress. Imagine if all the revenue of a country is spent on strengthening its defenses or engaging in war to either protect itself or expand its territory, where would there be scope for progress or the well being of its citizens?

Point to Ponder

Have you ever come across the term 'Peace Keeping Force'? Don't you think this is an oxymoron? Albert Einstein once said, "Peace cannot be kept by force; it can only be achieved by understanding." Why then do you think countries spend huge amounts of money on maintaining an army?

A VALUE FOR ME
"Peace begins with a smile."

Snippet

You can draw inspiration from any source. For many centuries, poets and bards have been writing and singing of peace. One such song sung by Paul Simon and Art Garfunkel, an American folk rock duo better known as Simon and Garfunkel, explicitly depicts the wonder of peace.

Read the lyrics below and listen to the song on the internet.

"Last Night I Had The Strangest Dream"

Last night I had the strangest dream
I ever dreamed before
I dreamed the world had all agreed
To put an end to war
I dreamed I saw a mighty room
The room was filled with men
And the paper they were signing said
They'd never fight again

And when the papers all were signed
And a million copies made
They all joined hands and bowed their heads
And grateful prayers were prayed
And the people in the streets below
Were dancing round and round
And guns and swords and uniforms
Were scattered on the ground

Last night I had the strangest dream
I ever dreamed before
I dreamed the world had all agreed
To put an end to war

Exercises

1. Solve the following crossword.

   All the sentences below talk about peace and its implications.

   1. People will feel more _____ (6)
   2. People will be _____ with each other (10)
   3. Inner peace will help us _____ better results (7)
   4. There will be no _____ (3)
   5. The world will be a _____ place. (7)
   6. The _____ used on wars, arms and ammunitions can be used to better the lives of people (5)
   7. There will be reduced _____ (9)
   8. Inner peace will keep us _____ (7)
   9. The _____, a bird, is also is considered the symbol of peace (4)
   10. Universally, _____ is the colour of peace (5)

2. Do you justify wars? Do you think that the arms and ammunition companies should be allowed in the world? Would the removal of all these companies lend to a more peaceful world? Express your views on the matter in **300** words.

3. **Paste pictures of any four people who have propagated peace. Write a few lines on what they have said about peace.**

Test yourself

Are you a cooperative person? Check for yourself by answering the following questions.

1. When someone talks ill of you,
    a. do you confront the person and talk it over? ☐
    b. do you also resort to talking ill of that person? ☐

2. How often do you get angry?
    a. Almost never ☐
    b. Frequently and quite easily ☐

3. What do you do when you get angry?
    a. Keep it to yourself ☐
    b. Take it out on something or someone ☐

4. What do you do when you come across an acquaintance in a mall?
    a. Smile and acknowledge them ☐
    b. Look at them and continue on my way ☐

5. While buying something, do you
    a. think of how it would affect someone (including you) ☐
    b. think of how it would benefit someone (including you) ☐

*If you have ticked on the boxes 1.a, 2.a, 3.a, 4.a, 5.a and 5.b, then you are a peaceful person. Congratulations. Else, you may want to practice to be more peaceful.

Tips to Parents and Teachers

They say, peaceful parents bring up peaceful kids. Hence, the first step to raising peaceful children is to ensure that you yourselves are peaceful human beings. The most essential thing that children need to be taught is tolerance. With tolerance comes acceptability. Children come to accept the differences in people, their thinking, their responses and their way of living. When they are able to know this, they can be peaceful.

Another way of ensuring that our children grow up to be peaceful citizens is to make them sensitive. While buying a product, let them ponder over how eco-friendly it is. Let them know of how the product is made and who makes the product. They can be made to appreciate hand crafted material and shun those that are made with illegal and inhuman practices such as child labour.

Dos and Don'ts

1. Find peace in Nature. Get away from the television and smart phones. Go out for a walk in a garden or a park. See the sights, take in the smells and find peace.
2. Help others. You will find peace when you interact in a friendly manner with others and help them.
3. Outer peace comes with inner peace. Meditate for a few minutes every day. You simply need to close your eyes and calm down.
4. Never resort to violence. If you are irritated or angry at someone, remain silent and count to ten or twenty before you react.
5. Positive thoughts help you in attaining peace.
6. Complete your tasks on time. A disciplined life will also help you attain peace.

> Peace begins with a smile.
> — Mother Teresa

Positivity

What is Positivity?
Positivity is the ability to think good thoughts. It is the ability to think well about any situation. It is the ability to be optimistic and not give in to pessimism or doubt. Positivity is also the ability to understand a situation properly and try to make the best out of it.
Thus, positivity is a way of thinking.

Read the following poem by Walter D Wintle, a poet from the early 20th century, to understand more about positivity.

The Man Who Thinks He Can

If you think you are beaten, you are;
If you think you dare not, you don't.
If you'd like to win, but think you can't
It's almost a cinch you won't.
If you think you'll lose, you've lost,
For out in the world we find
Success being with a fellow's will;
It's all in the state of mind.

If you think you're outclassed, you are:
You've got to think high to rise.
You've got to be sure of yourself before
You can ever win a prize.
Life's battles don't always go
To the stronger or faster man,
But soon or late the man who wins
Is the one who thinks he can.

—Walter D. Wintle

Comprehension questions

Answer the following questions to test your understanding of positivity.

1. According to the poem, what happens when you think you are beaten?
   _____
   _____
   _____

2. Explain the lines: 'If you'd like to win, but think you can't

   It's almost a cinch you won't.'
   _____
   _____
   _____

3. Why does the poet say that success is in the state of the mind?
   _____
   _____
   _____

4. How does being sure of yourself help you to win a prize?
   _____
   _____
   _____

5. Why does the poet say that 'life's battles don't always go to the stronger or the faster man'?
   _____
   _____
   _____

More about the Value

There are two ways of describing the glass with water.

Description 1: The glass is half-empty.

Description 2: The glass is half-full.

The half-empty / half-full glass is usually used to explain the concepts of optimism and pessimism. Have you ever thought that both the expressions can however be considered as positive outlooks depending on the situation you find yourself in?

For instance, of the glass contains a bitter concoction that you have to take as a medicine. You may despise the medicine and yet need to take it because it will make you better. Under such circumstances, you may ooze positivity if you see the glass as half-empty. It is a better way of looking at the situation. You can now congratulate yourself on drinking up half the bitter liquid and coax yourself to drink up the remaining half.

Now imagine, the glass was full of your favourite drink. Somebody spilt it. And what is remaining in the glass is what you see in the picture. You can think of the glass as half-full so that you may enjoy the remaining drink rather than feel bad about what you have lost.

Positivity, therefore, which is nothing but a more optimistic, cheerful and hopeful way you look at a situation will help you feel good about the situation and will enable you to make the best of it.

A VALUE FOR ME
"If you think you can do a thing, of you think you can't do a thing, you're always right."

Snippet

Once, a farmer's donkey fell into a dry well. The well was deep. The poor animal, naturally, out of fright brayed piteously. The farmer thought of ways to bring his animal out from the deep pit. However, he realized it was almost impossible to bring it out alive.

The only option that the farmer considered was to put an end to the donkey's misery. He decided to bury it alive in the well. He started shoveling in mud. Since the well was deep and a lot of mud needed to be thrown in, a few of his neighbours came to help the farmer.

The frightened donkey panicked even more when mud was being flung on it. It brayed louder. Each time a shovel full of mud was thrown on it, it shook its back vigorously. This continued for a while.

Can you guess what happened eventually?

Every time the donkey shook off the mud, it stepped over the new layer of mud on the floor of the well. With time, the well was almost filled with mud, but the donkey wasn't buried in it.

Eventually, the well was completely covered in mud, but the donkey stepped over the last pile of mud thrown in and gladly ran out of the well.

There is always a way out of seemingly impossible situations. The key is to think that you can find your way out, and search for that way till you come across it. Had the donkey remained still when the mud was being flung on it, it would have been buried alive.

> 'If you think you can do a thing, or you think you can't do a thing, you're always right.'
>
> — Henry Ford

Exercises

1. **Solve the following crossword. The clues below list out the benefits of being positive.**

    1. You are loved and _____ by people
    2. Positive _____
    3. Key to _____
    4. You become more _____
    5. Good _____
    6. Leads to _____
    7. _____ performance
    8. Will _____ you

9. _____ become opportunities
10. Reduced _____

2. **Which amongst the following Harry Potter Series characters show positivity? Put a tick or a cross against their names, as is applicable.**

   a. Albus Dumbledore – He is often found encouraging his students and colleagues.

   b. Severus Snape – He is always putting down and discouraging students. He is prejudiced.

   c. Neville Longbottom – He is never sure of himself. He is always underestimating himself.

   d. Hermione Granger – She has a 'never give up' attitude. No matter how difficult a task, she sees to it that she accomplishes it.

   e. Draco Malfoy – He is a cowardly bully who manipulates situations and people to get what he wants.

   f. Fred and George Weasley – They are mischievous and yet loyal to their friends. They make light of even somber situations. Their optimism and hard work make their joke shop a success.

3. The famous fable of the two frogs who jumped into the pot of milk is a classic example of positivity and its benefits. Write in your own words, how you can learn the value of positivity from this story.

_____
_____
_____
_____
_____
_____
_____
_____
_____
_____
_____

4. It is said the Thomas Alva Edison failed more than 1000 times when trying to create his famous light bulb. He later said, "I have not failed 1000 times. I have successfully discovered 1000 ways to not make a light bulb."

    What do you gather about positivity from this statement made by Edison? How will you apply it in your daily life?

_____
_____

_____
_____
_____
_____
_____
_____
_____
_____
_____

5. Create a poster to be put up in your classroom about positivity. You can make it as creative as possible by inserting slogans / poems / pictures / songs and so on.

> Keep your face to the sunshine and you will never see the shadow.
> — Helen Keller

Test yourself

1. When someone gives you a suggestion, you feel they are criticizing you. You do not like it.
2. When someone gives you a suggestion, you think about it and accept it. You see it as a way of improving yourself.
3. When you win something, you feel good about yourself. You know you won it because you were the best out there. There is no way anyone else can defeat you.
4. When you win something, you feel good about yourself. You know you won it because you were the best out there. You also know that you have to work very hard to remain the best.
5. When you come up with a suggestion that the others like, you are surprised at yourself. You think it is your lucky day where people accepted your suggestion. You don't know when such a day would come again in the future.

   If you have ticked sentences 1, 3 and 5, then you are not a very positive person. You may also be low on self-esteem. You need to work on positivity a bit more.

Tips to Parents and Teachers

Never voice negative thoughts in front of children. They tend to believe them over time. Likewise, never comment negatively. Comments such as "You are pathetic at Maths" will make the child believe it to be true. The child will then stop making an effort to improve and overcome the problem. Feedback should be as positive as possible. Encourage and motivate children with kind words. Children might come across depressing scenarios around them. Let them learn to observe the positive side of life along with these distressing situations.

Do's and Don'ts

1. Smile as much as you can, whenever you can. A smile costs nothing but helps you gain positivity.
2. Have friends who think positively. Their positivity can rub off on you. Likewise, if you are surrounded by people who think negatively, you too will start to have negative thoughts.
3. Singing, dancing and physical activities like exercises and games will help you develop positivity.
4. At the end of each day, list the things that you are grateful for.
5. Never dwell on negative thoughts and things for too long. They will drain away your energy.

> A man is but the product of his thoughts. What he thinks, he becomes.
> – Mahatma Gandhi, Indian leader

Compassion

What is compassion?

Compassion literally means 'suffer together'. It is the ability to sympathize with others who are suffering and then wanting to help them too. Many a times, we do not suffer physically. But we can feel the pain of someone else who is suffering. This ability to feel someone else's pain is called compassion. Compassion comes with a desire to help those who are suffering.

Compassion enables us to live peacefully, in a friendly manner and in harmony with others.

Let us read the following story to know more about compassion.

Story

The cherry blossoms are in full bloom at the Ueno Zoo. Their petals are falling in the soft breeze and sparkling in the sun. Beneath the cherry trees, crowds of people are pushing to enter the zoo on such a beautiful day. Two elephants are outside performing their tricks for a lively audience. While blowing the trumpets with their long trunks, the elephants walk along large wooden logs. Not far from the cheerful square, there stands a tombstone. Not many notice this monument for the animals that have died at the Ueno Zoo. It is quiet and peaceful here and the sun warms every corner.

One day, an employee of the zoo, while tenderly polishing the stone, told me the sad story of three elephants buried there. He said today there are three elephants in this zoo. But years ago, we had three different elephants here. Their names were John, Tonky and Wanly.

At that time, Japan was at war. Gradually, the war had become more and more severe. Bombs were dropped on Tokyo every day and night like falling rain. What would happen if the bombs hit the zoo? If the cages were broken and dangerous animals escaped to run wild through the city, it would be terrible! Therefore, by command of the Army, all the lions, tigers, leopards, bears and big snakes were poisoned to death.

By and by, the time came for the three elephants to be killed. They began with John. John loved potatoes, so the elephant keepers mixed poisoned potatoes with the good ones when it was time to feed him. John, however, was a very clever elephant. He ate the good potatoes, but each time he brought a poisoned potato to his mouth with his trunk, he would throw it to the ground.

"As it seems there is no other way," the zookeepers said, "we must inject poison directly into his body." A large syringe, the kind used to give shots to horses, was prepared. But John's skin was so tough that the big needles broke off with a loud snap one after the other. When this did not work, the keepers reluctantly decided to starve him to death. Poor John died seventeen days later.

Then it was Tonky's and Wanly's turn to die. These two had always gazed at people with loving eyes. They were sweet and gentle-hearted. The zookeepers wanted so much to keep Tonky and Wanly alive that they thought of sending them to the zoo in Sendai, far north of Tokyo. But what if bombs fell on Sendai? What if the elephants got loose and ran wild there? What would happen then? Tonky and Wanly too were doomed to be killed at the Ueno zoo, just like all the other animals.

The elephant keepers stopped feeding Tonky and Wanly. As the days passed, the elephants became thinner and thinner, weaker and weaker. Whenever a keeper walked by their cage, they would stand up, tottering, as if to beg, 'Give us something to eat. Please, give us water!' Their small, loving eyes began to look like round rubber balls in their drooping, shrunken faces. Their ears seemed too large for their bodies. The one big, strong elephants had become a sad shape.

All this while, the elephants' trainer loved them as if they were his own children. He could only pace in front of the cage and moan, 'You poor, poor, pitiful elephants!' One day, Tonky and Wanly lifted their heavy bodies, staggered to their feet, and came close to their trainer. Squeezing out what little strength they had left, Tonky and Wanly made their last appeal. They stood up on their hind legs and lifted their front legs up as high as they could. Then, raising their trunks high in the air, they did their banzai trick. Surely, their friend would reward them with food and water as he used to do.

The trainer could stand it no longer. 'Oh, Tonky! Oh, Wanly! he wailed, and dashed to the food shed. He carried food and pails of water to them and threw it at their feet. 'Here!' he said, sobbing, and clung to their thin legs. 'Eat your food! Please drink. Drink your water!'

All of the other keepers pretended not to see what the trainer had done. No one said a word. The director of the zoo just sat very still, biting his lip and gazing at the top of his desk. No one was supposed to give the elephants any food. No one was supposed to give them any water. But everyone was hoping and praying that if the elephants could survive only one more day, the war might be over and the elephants would be saved.

At last, Tonky and Wanly could not move. They just lay on their sides, hardly able to see the white clouds floating in the sky over the zoo. However, their eyes appeared clearer and more beautiful than ever. Seeing his beloved elephants dying this way, the elephant trainer felt as if his heart would break. He had no more courage to see them. All of the other keepers felt the same, and they too stayed away from the elephants' cage.

Over two weeks later, Tonky and Wanly were dead. Both died leaning against the bars of their cage with their trunks stretched high in the air, still trying to do their banzai trick for the people who once fed them. 'The elephants are dead! They're dead!' screamed the elephant trainer as he ran into the office. He buried his head in his arms and cried, beating the desktop with his fist. The rest of the zoo keepers ran to the elephants' cage and stumbled in. They took hold of Tonky and Wanly's thin bodies, as if to shake them back to life. Everyone burst into tears, then stroked the elephants' legs and trunks in sorrow.

Above them, in the bright blue sky, the angry roar of enemy planes returned. Bombs began to drop on Tokyo once more. Still clinging to the elephants, the zookeepers raised their fists to the sky and implored, 'Stop the war! Stop all wars!'

Later, when the bodies of the elephants were examined nothing was found in their washtub like stomachs - not even one drop of water. With tears in his eyes, the zookeeper finished his story. "These three elephants - John, Tonky and Wanly - are now resting peacefully under this monument." He was still patting the tombstone tenderly as the cherry blossoms fell on the grave like snowflakes.

Faithful Elephants (A True Story of Animals, People and War)

—Yukio Tsuchiya

Comprehension questions

Answer the following questions to check your understanding of the story.

1. Where and in which country is the story of the Faithful Elephants placed?

   _____
   _____
   _____

2. In whose honour is the tomb constructed at the Tokyo zoo?

   _____
   _____
   _____

3. Why was it decided that the three elephants along with the other dangerous animals of the zoo were to be killed?
   _____
   _____
   _____

4. What were the various methods employed to kill the elephants?
   _____
   _____
   _____

5. Why did the zookeeper disobey the orders and give the elephants food one day?
   _____
   _____
   _____

6. Why did the people at the zoo wish for the war to end?
   _____
   _____
   _____

More about the Value

Have you ever wondered why is it essential to develop the quality of compassion?

When you are able to understand the suffering of others and when you are able to feel the pain of others, you will be able to help them better. Also, you will refrain from doing any such act that will cause pain and suffering to others.

Today, terrorism is a major concern in almost every corner of the world. When a terror attack is carried out on the people of some country that you have never visited, you feel their pain, don't you? You are thankful that you weren't in that country or at that place during the terror attack. You are also fearful that the attack could be in your country and in your city. This fear, the pain and the ability to wish that such a thing should never happen to anyone is compassion.

If you are a compassionate person, you will never intentionally harm anyone. Therefore, compassion is extremely essential.

Also, any relief measure sent during a natural calamity is done out of compassion. If you were the one stranded in floods without any food or medicines, you would be extremely glad for the help offered by others when they fly in food packets and essential medicines. It is then that you would be happy for the compassionate nature of others.

Compassion makes our world a better place. It makes people feel warm and friendly.

A VALUE FOR ME

Compassion is never forgotten. It changes the world and makes it a better place.

Snippet

In 1892, a Stanford University student was struggling to pay his fees. He was an orphan, had no one to fund his education, and had to pay his fees himself. He then came up with an idea. Along with a friend of his, he decided to have a musical concert at campus. The money he would collect would fund his education.

The two young men invited the great pianist Ignacy J. Paderewski for the concert. The pianist charged $2000 per recital and the young men agreed to pay the amount.

However, the men could not sell enough tickets for the concert. They managed to collect only $1600. They explained the situation to the pianist. They apologized for the inconvenience they had caused the great man and then handed over all the money they had collected through selling the tickets. They wrote him a cheque for the remaining $400, even though they were broke and had their college fees to pay too.

Paderewski refused the money. He tore up the cheque and returned the $1600 dollars to the young men. He said, "Deduct all the money that you have spent in arranging for this concert. Keep whatever you need for your fees. And if there is anything left, you can give it to me."

The men were surprised and thrilled. They thanked the pianist and left.

Years later, Paderewski became the Prime Minister of Poland. When the World War began, Poland was devastated. Over 1.5 million people were starving in that country. The Prime Minister sought help from the Unites States of America.

The person who was contacted was Herbert Hoover. Incidentally, Hoover later became the President of USA. He arranged for large shipments of food grains to be transported to Poland. Paderewski later went over USA to personally thank Hoover for the help he had offered to Poland.

When the two met, Hoover said, "You shouldn't be thanking me. I was one of the persons you had helped a long time ago to get through college. I was one of the two students who had approached you for a concert where you refused to charge us the money we promised you."

This is a true story that had happened in 1892 at Stanford University.

Compassion is never forgotten. It changes the world and makes it a better place.

Exercises

1. Who among the following people would you say are compassionate?

   a. Mother Teresa  She lived to serve the poor and the suffering.

   b. Adolph Hitler  Founder and leader of the Nazi Party that was responsible for the Holocaust.

   c. Osama Bin Laden  Founder of the al-Qaeda, the organization that was responsible for the 9/11 terror attacks and many others.

   d. Dalai Lama  The spiritual leader of the Tibetan people, he helps spread the word of the Buddha.

   e. Abraham Lincoln  Considered to be one of the most influential American Presidents. His famous speech inspired the entire nation to bring about the abolishment of slavery.

2. Mention ways in which you would want to help the poor in the world and bring about a difference in their life. Read out to your classmates what you have listed. Discuss and debate if these methods are proper.

_____
_____
_____
_____
_____
_____
_____

3. Given below is a news report. Read it up and then write a pamphlet requesting help as relief to the people affected. In your pamphlet, you need to mention briefly about the calamity and then list out ways in which people can help.

Severe Weather in Chennai, India Kills 55

Severe weather in Chennai and other parts of Tamil Nadu has claimed lives of at least 55 people including 27 in Cuddalore district alone.

According to regional meteorological centre, a low pressure area formed over the Bay of Bengal caused the downpour in the area.

Nungambakkam and Meenambakkam in Chennai received 15 cm and 11.7cm of rainfall respectively on Thursday night. Kancheepuram recorded 34 cm rainfall.

4. **Which of the following would you say are gestures of compassion?**

   a. Offering condolences ☐

   b. Being Grateful ☐

   c. Showing derision ☐

   d. Criticizing ☐

   e. Offering help ☐

   f. Congratulating someone ☐

   g. Bullying others ☐

   h. Turning a blind eye to someone's suffering because it does not concern us ☐

   i. Offering charity ☐

   j. Showing mercy ☐

   k. Sympathizing with others ☐

5. **Activity: What is your view about _____?**

   a. Bullying:

   b. Sharing:

   c. Anger:

   d. Gossip:

   e. Rumors:

   f. Listening:

   Do you think any of these help or prevent in building the ability to be compassionate? How do they help or don't help in becoming compassionate?

   _____
   _____
   _____
   _____
   _____
   _____
   _____
   _____
   _____

Test yourself

Take the following test to find out how compassionate you are.

1. Do you like to share your knowledge with others?
2. When your friend wins a prestigious award, do you feel jealous?
3. Do you believe in expressing gratitude? Do you thank those who help you and return the favour whenever you can?
4. When there is news of a disaster like an earthquake or a tsunami on TV, do you switch it off or change to another channel because you are feeling depressed by the news?

5. When you see someone in your school crying, who is not a close friend, do you avoid going near him/her?

*If your answers to questions 1 and 3 are 'yes' then you are a compassionate person.

A compassionate person will be able to share the joy of a person as well as feel his or her pain. Therefore, if you feel jealous over a friend's achievements, you are not exactly a compassionate person.

If you think that you have switched off the TV or changed to another channel because you can feel the pain of the people who suffered in the natural disaster and cannot bear to watch their suffering anymore, you may not exactly be compassionate. A compassionate person would understand the pain and suffering of the people and go on to find a way to help them.

You may be a shy person. You may not be in the habit of speaking to many in your school. However, if you are a compassionate person and you see someone, especially from your school crying, you would walk up to that person and ask what the matter is. You would also try and help that person.

Tips to Parents and Teachers

Teach children to share and donate. A self-centered child is generally incapable of empathy (the ability to understand another person's pain) and compassion (the ability to understand another person's pain and a yearning to help alleviate that pain.) Teach the child to share the joys and sorrows of his or her friends. Courtesies like wishing a person on his birthday or at the start of a new venture; conveying condolences and expressing grief over someone else's loss have to be taught to children. This will help the child to learn to empathize.

Teach them to respect everyone and make them understand that every person has the right to live with dignity.

Do's and Don'ts

1. When you see someone suffering, you should be able to understand their suffering and think of ways in which you can help alleviate that suffering.
2. Remember to treat everyone with respect and kindness. Never be rude to anyone.
3. Be positive. You can only help others when you are calm and with hope.
4. Look for the similarities rather than differences between yourself and others.
5. Take pleasure in helping others.

Determination

What is determination?
Determination is the ability of a person to do something till it is completed. It is the ability to see the task to its completion despite the number of obstacles faced and despite the difficulty of the task. Determination is the intent of completing a task.
Determination is one of the most important qualities for success.

Let us read the following story to know more about determination.

Story

Somewhere in one of the forests of India, there lived a tiny sparrow. The forests were the home of the sparrow, its family and many other creatures. There was always plenty of food, shelter and water for the living things in this forest.

Sadly, however, a forest fire burnt down this entire lush green forest. Fate was such that only the tiny sparrow survived. Saddened by the fate of its family and friends, it decided to fly to a new place to begin a new life among new friends.

While flying, it spotted some lentils. They were the only bits of food it found in a long time. The land was suffering a famine and food and water were scarce to come by. The sparrow ate to its full. There was another seed remaining. The sparrow decided to carry it in its beak, and save it for later.

While flying over a city, the seed fell out of the sparrow's beak and got lodged in a narrow slit in a log. The sparrow was devastated. It wasn't sure when it would get food again. It wanted its food back.

Nearby was a man walking with an axe in his hand. He looked like a carpenter in search of wood for some furniture. The sparrow approached the man and said,

"Carpenter! Can you please help me dear man?

Will you slit the log so that I may take my food?"

The carpenter stared incredulously at the sparrow and replied,

"Do I need to waste my effort to help you,

A poor feeble sparrow?

No, I won't slit the log."

Saying so, he walked on.

The bird was angered. How can he refuse to help a fellow living thing who is in need? Let me complain to the king, it thought. On finding the king of the place, the sparrow said,

"Mighty king! I seek justice.

Please reprimand the carpenter who refused to slit the log

In which my precious lentil is lodged."

The King spoke with indifference,

"Do I, the King,

Waste my time in reprimanding a carpenter

Who refused to help you dislodge a mere lentil?

Leave, I will do no such thing."

The sparrow did not give up. It approached the Queen, for who better to convince the King than his wife. On finding the Queen in the palace, the sparrow said,

"Honourable Queen, please plead my case with the King,

Who refused to reprimand the carpenter

Who refused to slit the log to retrieve my lost lentil."

The Queen could not be bothered with such trivial things.

"Go! I will not plead with the King

To talk to the carpenter

To slit the log

To retrieve you lentil."

The sparrow next went to a snake.

"Snake! I am so angered by the Queen

Who refused to speak to the King

Who refused to reprimand the carpenter

Who refused to help me get back my lentil.

Please threaten to bite her."

As you can guess by now, the snake too refused. The sparrow, determined even more than before next approached a stick. It asked the stick to beat up the snake for refusing to help it. The stick too did not budge an inch to help the bird. The sparrow then approached fire. "Will you please threaten to burn up the stick?" it asked. But the fire too refused.

Finally, when the bird approached water, the cool water heard the sparrow's misery. It promised to help the bird. The water then went on to threaten to put out the fire for refusing to help the sparrow.

The fire panicked. It apologized and went on to threaten the stick.

The stick now scared of getting scarred, or worse, burnt, went on to threaten the snake.

The snake slid as fast as it could, away from the stick and approached the Queen.

The Queen realized that the snake was helping the sparrow. Avoiding getting bitten by the snake, the Queen ran up to the King and convinced him to talk to the carpenter.

The King summoned the carpenter and ordered him to help the sparrow.

Eventually, after such a lot of effort, the sparrow got back its precious lentil.

Weak and timid we may be, yet our determination will lead us to success.

Comprehension questions

Answer the following questions to check your understanding of the story.

1. Why was the sparrow flying to a new forest?
   _____
   _____
   _____

2. Why was food scarce to come by for the sparrow?
   _____
   _____
   _____

3. Why do you think the people, animals and things in the story refused to help the sparrow?

   _____
   _____
   _____

4. What were the various reasons because of which the people, things and animals started helping the sparrow?

   _____
   _____
   _____

5. Name any two qualities of the sparrow (apart from its determination) that you gather from this story.

   _____
   _____
   _____

More about the Value

When you have a task to do, and you find it difficult, you have two options in front of you.

Option 1: Give up the task.

Option 2: Work harder, find a solution, sweat it out and finish the task.

Which one would you choose?

Giving up is easy. It is akin to escaping doing a work. It is the mark of a weak person; a person who is not ambitious or determined. On the hand, if you push yourself to work harder, you may find it momentarily difficult. However, the happiness and the contentment you feel when you complete the task is indescribable.

There have been many instances when people gave up tasks when the going got tough. However, it is those people who had gone beyond those hardships and worked with focus that became successful.

> "Never stop. One stops as soon as something is about to happen."
> — Peter Brock

Read the following true story of Glenn Cunningham to understand why determination is important.

A VALUE FOR ME

"Our greatest glory is not in never falling but in rising every time we fall."

Snippet

Somewhere in America was a little boy named Glenn Cunningham. Glenn would come in early to school to start the kerosene stove that heated his classroom. The kerosene stove was the only way the teacher and the children could remain warm in the harsh winters.

One morning, the teacher and the children arrived at school to find it engulfed in flames. They realized that Glenn must be trapped inside. Some braved to enter the building and dragged poor Glenn out.

Glenn was badly burnt. The doctors gave up hope on Glenn. They thought he would die. But Glenn didn't. The doctors told the boy's mother that it was better the poor boy died because he was so badly burnt that living would be a nightmare for him. His lower body was so burnt that he would not be able to use his legs ever. He would remain a scarred cripple.

Glenn not only did not want to die, but he also did not want to remain a cripple. His parents diligently massaged his legs every day. Try as they might, they could not get any sensation or movement in Glenn's legs.

Glenn was still determined not to remain a cripple. His mother would take him out into the garden every day after the massage and leave him there for a while in the open air. One day, Glenn simply threw himself off the wheel chair and dragged himself to the picket fence around his house. With great effort he pulled himself up against the fence and started dragging his lifeless legs and his body around the house taking the support of the fence.

He did this every day. Such was his determination that he not only managed to drag himself around, he eventually started walking with support, since he was then able to move his legs again. Such was his perseverance that he was later able to walk around even without support.

If you think the boy who was considered as good as dead by the doctors miraculously managed to live and walk again, you would be surprised that he started running too. He not only ran but ran to create records. He was also given the nickname 'Kansas Flyer'.

Exercises

1. **True or False**

    a. Being determined is extremely easy. _____

    b. Determination comes with being able to control our emotions and desires. _____

    c. Determination means doing something without giving up midway. _____

    d. If you are determined, it means that you have the ability to decide what you can or cannot do. Therefore, you never take up any task which is difficult for you. _____

    e. When you are determined, you have your doubts, but you don't give in to them. You face the challenge no matter how difficult it is. _____

    f. You may not always have people to help you or stand by you when you are determined. You may be fighting your battles or causes all by yourself. Therefore, you need a lot of mental strength to be determined. _____

2. **Pick from the list below the character traits that are generally shown by determined people. Write them down in the box provided.**

Determined people

boring	always serious	proud
intolerant	clumsy	good at solving problems
careless	self-disciplined	active
on their toes	focused	hardworking

unkind   shrewd   sophisticated

trusting   frugal   experimental

dishonest   childish

3. Match the following characters to their actions.

	Characters	Their Actions
a.	Sherlock Holmes	bites the apple offered by the old woman though she had been warned by the dwarves not to accept anything from strangers.
b.	Bhishma	endured the tough life of the jungles for 14 years to keep his word.
c.	Snow White	finds it easy to lie his way through.
d.	Pandora	sticks to his promise to not marry and take care of the family and the heirs to the throne for as long as he lives.
e.	Rama	is slow and yet steady in running the race through to the end.
f.	Pinocchio	strives to see the end of a case and solve the mystery surrounding it, no matter how difficult it may be.
g.	Tortoise	opens the box because she is not able to contain her curiosity.

Based on their actions mentioned above, which of these characters do you think were determined?

_____
_____
_____
_____
_____

Test yourself

Take the following test to check if you are a determined person.

1. When you are in pain, what do you do?

    a. Look for a way to overcome the pain with a pain relief balm or a medicine or some other way ☐

    b. Cry and seek the attention of people around you, hoping that they would comfort you ☐

2. If you have to decide between eating your favourite chocolate and staying away from it because your mother told you to, what would you do?

    a. Refrain from eating it, however tempting it may be ☐

    b. Eat it, assuming that your mother would not get to know of it ☐

3. Imagine you are living on the 21st floor of a building. The lift suddenly went out of service. You have to get to school immediately because your football team is waiting for you. What will you do?

    a. Call up your school and inform them that you cannot make it to practice ☐

    b. Climb down all the 21 floors considering it a warm up exercise and eventually get to school ☐

4. You are at a market. You have already spent most of your money on some sports shoes that you have wanted for a long time. Later, when you are about to leave the market, you come across your favourite video game. What do you do?

    a. Buy it because you like it ☐

    b. Consider the fact that you have already spent a huge amount on shoes and hence tell yourself that you should go away without purchasing the game ☐

5. What do you do when you are unable to solve a math problem?

    a. Wait for the teacher to explain it ☐

    b. Search the internet for a way to solve the problem or ask your friends or teacher to help you with it ☐

*If your answers are 1.a, 2.a, 3.a, 4.b and 5.b then you show signs of being a determined person.

Tips to Parents and Teachers

Determination has to be nurtured in children. Encourage them to complete a task that they have begun. Praise them when they have done the work. A word of praise is a good motivation. When children find themselves in difficult situations, encourage them to complete the work or overcome the situation but do not help them unless the situation really needs it. Failure is a stepping-stone to success. When children fail at a task, let them not get disheartened and leave the job midway. Encourage them to take up the work once again and do it better this time so that they may succeed at it.

Do's and Don'ts

1. Know your strengths. Know your limitations as well.
2. Set yourself goals. Work to achieve these goals.
3. Do not stop with setting easily achievable goals. Push yourself. Once you know your strengths and your limitations and learn to push yourself, you will be surprised how much you can achieve.
4. Never get disheartened by failure. Treat every failure as a chance to learn from them.
5. Think positively.
6. Be responsible for your actions and your behaviour.

> "Our greatest glory is not in never falling but in rising every time we fall."
> — Confucius

Open Mindedness

What is open mindedness?
Being open to suggestions and new ideas is open mindedness. It is the ability to be tolerant towards others, their views and their outlook. It is also the ability to listen to others patiently. Open mindedness opens windows to innovation, growth and over all development.

Let us read the following poem by John Godfrey Saxe to understand more about the value.

The Blind Men and the Elephant

It was six men of Hindustan

To learning much inclined,

Who went to see the Elephant

(Though all of them were blind),

That each by observation

Might satisfy his mind.

The First approach'd the Elephant,

And happening to fall

Against his broad and sturdy side,

At once began to bawl:

"God bless me! but the Elephant

Is very like a wall!"

The Second, feeling of the tusk,

Cried, -"Ho! what have we here

So very round and smooth and sharp?

To me 'tis mighty clear

This wonder of an Elephant

Is very like a spear!"

The Third approached the animal,

And happening to take

The squirming trunk within his hands,

Thus boldly up and spake:

"I see," quoth he, "the Elephant

Is very like a snake!"

The Fourth reached out his eager hand,

And felt about the knee.

"What most this wondrous beast is like

Is mighty plain," quoth he,

"'Tis clear enough the Elephant

Is very like a tree!"

The Fifth, who chanced to touch the ear,

Said: "E'en the blindest man

Can tell what this resembles most;

Deny the fact who can,

This marvel of an Elephant

Is very like a fan!"

The Sixth no sooner had begun

About the beast to grope,

Then, seizing on the swinging tail

That fell within his scope,

"I see," quoth he, "the Elephant

Is very like a rope!"

And so these men of Indostan

Disputed loud and long,

Each in his own opinion

Exceeding stiff and strong,

Though each was partly in the right,

And all were in the wrong!

— John Godfrey Saxe

Had the six men been willing to listen to each other's description of the elephant and attempted to understand what the other person was saying, they would all have had a fair idea of what an elephant looks like.

Comprehension questions

Answer the following questions to check your understanding of the story.

1. Why did the six men of Indostan go to see the elephant?
   _____
   _____
   _____

2. Why did each of the six men have different ideas of what an elephant looks like?
   _____
   _____
   _____

3. On feeling the tusk of the elephant, what did the second man compare an elephant to?
   _____
   _____
   _____

4. What were the different things the blind men compared the elephant to?
   _____
   _____
   _____

5. Do you think the blind men from Indostan were open-minded? Explain.
   _____
   _____
   _____

More about the Value

Open mindedness does not imply that one agrees with the views of the others. On the contrary, it is the ability to listen to another person without interrupting him or her. It is the ability to understand the other perspective.

Once you have listened and understood the other person, you are at liberty to compare and contrast your views with theirs and choose wisely whether to stick to your own views, discard yours and accept the other viewpoint or amalgamate the two.

Open mindedness is essential for a peaceful and harmonious society. The world is a diverse place. Its people are diverse in their habitats and their cultures. Yet, they are closer than never before with the onset of modern technology. It is imperative that we all learn to be open-minded so that we may be tolerant, understanding and accepting of people from different parts of the world. This is what will ensure there is no conflict or war in the world.

Open mindedness is also the key to scientific growth and development. Without being open minded, it is impossible for the advancement of science and technology. In short, open mindedness is the key to a better future.

A VALUE FOR ME
Intolerance stems from the inability to be open-minded.

Snippet

A young man in his early twenties and his father were travelling in a train. An elderly couple were travelling in the same coach alongside the father and son. A little into the journey, the son said out loud, "Father, do you see the trees are going behind us!" His enthusiasm was that of a small boy who was on his first train journey. He was loud, chirpy and eagerly looking out of the window of the coach not missing out on any of the view outside.

A little while later, with equal gusto, he shouted, "Father, the clouds are travelling with us! They are running along with the train."

The couple sitting next to the young man and his father were perplexed by the man's childish comments. Thinking him to be mentally challenged, they looked at him with pity and advised the man's father, "Why don't you take your son to a good doctor?"

The father smiled and replied, "I did. In fact, we are returning from the hospital. My son was blind from birth and he got his eyes just this week."

This story teaches us to be open minded about situations, people and their behaviour. Appearances can be deceptive. Every person would have his or her own perspective on things and reason for his or her behaviour. One should develop the ability to fully understand a situation after getting to know all the facts before arriving at any conclusion.

Exercises

1. Given below are some traits commonly found in many. Group them in columns A and B according to whether or not they contribute to open-mindedness in people.

Jealousy	Hatred	Compassion	Helpfulness
Patience	Anger	Impatience	Confidence
Respect	Tolerance	Pride	Willingness to learn
Annoyance	Acceptance	Bitterness	Defiance
Disgust		Vanity	

Column A
Traits that lend to open mindedness
_____
_____
_____
_____
_____

Column B
Traits that do not lend to open mindedness
_____
_____
_____
_____
_____

2. **Research Work:** Select any five cultures of the world. Let them be as varied as possible. Do some research on the people from these cultures. You could cover topics like their language, their attire, their beliefs and so on. Choose one aspect that strikes you most from each culture. Think a bit more about this aspect. Find out why or how this aspect has come to be. For instance, you may find the wooden shoes of the Dutch very fascinating. Find out why the wooden shoes are made and why they are so popular. Likewise, you may find the doll festival of Japan intriguing. Find out why this festival is celebrated. Paste pictures if possible to make your work even more interesting. Share your findings and your thoughts with your friends. Bring about a positive comparison between these aspects and any other you know if you can.

No.	What I found interesting (draw or paste a picture)	What it is called and where it is from	How it is fascinating!	The similarities and the contrasts
1.				
2.				
3.				
4.				
5.				
6.				

3. **Supply a word. Each of the following sentences will then elucidate ways in which you can exercise open-mindedness.**

> Music   Change   Language   Listen   Cuisine
> Judging   Strategy   Mysteries

a. Learn a new _____.

b. Try out a new _____.

c. Play games like chess, checkers and so on that involve _____.

d. Spend some time thinking about the _____ of the world.

e. Listen to new kinds of _____.

f. _____ to another person when he or she speaks.

g. Put yourself in the other person's shoes before _____ them.

h. Be ready for _____. Accept it as a challenge and an adventure.

4. **Who among the following would you say is open-minded?**

a. Mehek doesn't want to travel by the local train in Mumbai. She hasn't seen them yet but has heard that they are very crowded. _____

b. Kiran, Mehek's sister has also never seen or travelled by the Mumbai local trains. She is however, curious to experience the travel by these famous trains. _____

c. Manish is afraid to make friends with a person from Pakistan. After all, his country and Pakistan are supposed to be not so friendly. _____

d. Sam tastes the local cuisine of every place he visits. It is another matter that he doesn't like everything he has tasted. _____

e. Sara doesn't play with everyone in her street. She prefers to play with only those children who go to her own school. _____

f. While constructing the new building, the architects and the builders have allowed for a huge garden around it. They propose to grow fruit bearing trees in the garden. They will also construct a huge birdbath with fresh water filled in it every day. _____

g. In his speech, the city mayor has asked for suggestions from all the people in the city to help clear it of its garbage. He also said that he was open to new ideas to make the city a cleaner place. _____

5. Open-mindedness comes with listening, seeing and understanding. The first step therefore is to observe without passing any comment. Listening is part of this first step. As children, we are taught to listen to our elders. We are taught to first let the other person speak and then reply only when the other person has completed what he or she is saying. It is rude to interrupt someone while they are speaking.

Also, it is essential that one listens with both the ears open.

Here is an activity that will help you practice listening. Divide the entire class into two groups. Next, come up with around 10 topics on which you can speak. Write down these topics on bits of paper and place them in a jar or a bowl. Children from one group will take turn in picking up a topic and then will speak on it. The rest of the class is supposed to listen to the child speaking. Once the speaker has finished what he or she has to say, a child from the other group will have to repeat what the speaker has said. You could begin by saying, "From what I understand, …." Or "From what you have said, I gather….".

Test yourself

Take the following test to check if you are an open-minded person.

1. A person you don't like has asked you for help in a school project. You

    a. refuse to help because you don't like that person

    b. help just because you can help in the project

2. Do you like trying out new things like new cuisines, new books and so on?

3. If you are asked to play the character of a donkey in a school play, will you

    a. turn it down because you think it is demeaning

    b. accept the role and think of ways in which you can be a convincing donkey

4. Do you make friends on the basis of their

    a. language, religion, etc.

    b. character

5. Your best friend wants to play cricket. You have never played the game. Do you

    a. agree to play but first ask the friend to explain all the rules to you properly

    b. refuse to play

*If you have ticked 1.b, 3.b, 4.b, 5.a and answered question 2 with a 'yes' then you are an open-minded person.

Tips to Parents and Teachers

Open mindedness comes with exposure to different cultures. Talk to children about the diversities in the world. Make your talk positive. Help them to nurture their curiosity about different cultures. Encourage them to learn a new language.

Never stop them from making friends with people from a different background or culture. Teach them that while nothing in the world is perfect, things are not imperfect either. Explain how people act or behave the way they do because of circumstances.

Let them learn to see beyond what is visible and delve into what motivated a particular action or comment from someone.

And of course, open mindedness too, like many other values comes with observation and imitation. Therefore, be open minded yourself and refrain from making negative comments about people, their thoughts and their culture.

Do's and Don'ts

1. Respect everyone.
2. While you may not agree with some people in most situations, there is no need to prove the other person wrong or bring them over to your way of thinking.
3. Be ready for change. Accept change. Enjoy change.
4. Learn about new cultures. Learn a new language or two.
5. Never miss out an opportunity to see new places.
6. Learn to think logically.
7. Don't get carried away by what another person says. Learn to think for yourself.
8. Listen to people. There is a lot of wisdom to be learnt from everyone.

> Intolerance stems from the inability to be open-minded.

Analyzing Myself   (Introspection Time)

Take time to think about yourself. Answer the following questions with sincerity.

1. What according to you is your greatest achievement to date?

   _____
   _____
   _____
   _____
   _____

2. What according to you is your greatest failure to date?

   _____
   _____
   _____
   _____
   _____

3. What is your greatest strength?

   _____
   _____
   _____
   _____
   _____

4. What is your greatest weakness?

   _____
   _____
   _____
   _____
   _____

5. If you were to point out one thing that others can do to make you happy, what would it be?

   _____
   _____
   _____

6. What is the one thing that you would do to make others happy?
   _____
   _____
   _____
   _____
   _____

7. If you were given immense power for a year, what would you do to better our society?
   _____
   _____
   _____
   _____
   _____

8. Imagine a fairy godmother or a wizard is watching over you. He or she will ensure that whatever you do becomes a success. What are the activities that you would undertake?
   _____
   _____
   _____
   _____
   _____